Paris Fashion Designs
1912–1913
COLORING BOOK

In 1912 and 1913, Paris fashion designs for women were high waisted, long sleeved, floor length, and often made of flimsy, see-through material. Dress silhouettes were wide at the hips and very narrow at the ankle. Fashionable clothing was only for the rich, because it was expensive and impossible to work in, and although beautiful, a lot of it was extremely uncomfortable to wear. To squeeze into fashionable outfits, women wore long girdles, which made it difficult to sit down. Some skirts were so narrow at the knees that the wearer could only take tiny steps. Imagine running for a bus or taxi in those clothes! Even getting into and out of a car would be nearly impossible.

Coats were cocoon-like or kimono shaped. Fur coats and stoles were very popular, and women often carried a huge matching hand warmer, called a *muff*. Cloth coats were edged with fur, too—fox, otter, chinchilla, mink, rabbit, and even squirrel and skunk fur. Women also wore striking but rather ridiculous hats—some turban-like, some shaped like lampshades, and others festooned with ostrich, peacock, or other large feathers.

In the early twentieth century, there were no high-fashion models, runway shows, or glossy women's magazines with gossip about celebrities. The first Paris fashion magazines featured hand-colored prints like the ones displayed on the inside covers of this coloring book. When you fill in the twenty-two line drawings, have fun choosing dramatic color schemes, and daydream a bit about what it would be like to wear these elegant, but oh so impractical, clothes. We've left the last page of the book blank so that you can draw and color an outfit of your own design.

Pomegranate

Original works of art are from the collection of the Glasgow Museums. The line drawings in this coloring book are details of prints by the following artists:

1. Armand Vallée (French, 1884–1960), Glasgow Museums SP.2009.3.29
2. Loeze (dates unknown), Glasgow Museums SP.2009.3.48
3. Armand Vallée (French, 1884–1960), Glasgow Museums SP.2009.3.14
4. Robert Pichenot (dates unknown), Glasgow Museums SP.2009.3.25
5. Maurice Taquoy (French, 1878–1952), Glasgow Museums SP.2009.3.23
6. Jan van Brock (dates unknown), Glasgow Museums SP.2009.3.57
7. George Barbier (French, 1882–1932), Glasgow Museums SP.2009.3.28
8. Mfn (artist unknown), Glasgow Museums SP.2009.3.19
9. Armand Vallée (French, 1884–1960), Glasgow Museums SP.2009.3.34
10. B. Berty (dates unknown), Glasgow Museums SP.2009.3.51
11. George Barbier (French, 1882–1932), Glasgow Museums SP.2009.3.40
12. Artist unknown, Glasgow Museums SP.2009.3.36
13. Jan van Brock (dates unknown), Glasgow Museums SP.2009.3.53
14. Victor Lhuer (French, dates unknown), Glasgow Museums SP.2009.3.47
15. Charles Martin (French, 1848–1934), Glasgow Museums SP.2009.3.18
16. George Barbier (French, 1882–1932), Glasgow Museums SP.2009.3.11
17. Aris Metzanos (dates unknown), Glasgow Museums SP.2009.3.30
18. Mfn (artist unknown), Glasgow Museums SP.2009.3.45
19. George Barbier (French, 1882–1932), Glasgow Museums SP.2009.3.21
20. Charles Martin (French, 1884–1934), Glasgow Museums SP.2009.3.38
21. Lucien Robert (dates unknown), Glasgow Museums SP.2009.3.42
22. H. Robert Dammy (dates unknown), Glasgow Museums SP.2009.3.26

Pomegranate Communications, Inc.
19018 NE Portal Way, Portland OR 97230
800 227 1428   www.pomegranate.com

Pomegranate Europe Ltd.
Unit 1, Heathcote Business Centre, Hurlbutt Road
Warwick, Warwickshire CV34 6TD, UK
[+44] 0 1926 430111
sales@pomeurope.co.uk

Catalog No. CB139

Designed and rendered by Susan Koop

Printed in Korea

24 23 22 21 20 19 18 17 16 15   12 11 10 9 8 7 6 5 4

2

3

7

8

9

AIMÉ

10

14

12

16

17

18

19

24

22

Draw and color your own picture here!